HEROIC ANIMALS
TOGO TAKES LEAD
HEROIC SLED DOG OF THE ALASKA SERUM RUN

BY **BRUCE BERGLUND**   ILLUSTRATED BY **DANTE GINEVRA**

CAPSTONE PRESS
a capstone imprint

Published by Capstone Press, an imprint of Capstone.
1710 Roe Crest Drive, North Mankato, Minnesota 56003
capstonepub.com

Library of Congress Cataloging-in-Publication Data
Names: Berglund, Bruce R., author. | Ginevra, Dante, 1976- illustrator.
Title: Togo takes the lead : heroic sled dog of the Alaska serum run / by Bruce Berglund ; illustrated by Dante Ginevra.
Description: North Mankato, Minnesota : Capstone Press, [2023] | Series: Heroic animals | Includes bibliographical references. | Audience: Ages 8-11 | Audience: Grades 4-6
Summary: "In January 1925, many people in Nome, Alaska, and the surrounding area were sick and dying from an outbreak of diphtheria. A supply of medicine was found but there was one problem-it was hundreds of miles away. The only way to get it to Nome was by dogsled. Ride along with the heroic sled dog Togo and his owner, Leonhard Sepalla, as they make a dangerous journey across Alaska's unforgiving wilderness to deliver lifesaving medicine to the people of Nome"-- Provided by publisher.
Identifiers: LCCN 2022024622 (print) | LCCN 2022024623 (ebook) | ISBN 9781666393989 (hardcover) | ISBN 9781666394221 (paperback) | ISBN 9781666393972 (pdf) | ISBN 9781666394245 (kindle edition)
Subjects: LCSH: Togo (Dog), 1913-1929--Juvenile literature. | Siberian husky--Alaska--Nome--Biography--Juvenile literature. | Sled dogs--Alaska--Nome--Biography--Juvenile literature. | Mushers--Alaska--Nome--Juvenile literature. | Diphtheria--Alaska--Nome--Juvenile literature. | Diphtheria antitoxin--Juvenile literature.
Classification: LCC SF429.S65 B47 2023 (print) | LCC SF429.S65 (ebook) | DDC 636.7309798/6--dc23/eng/20220822
LC record available at https://lccn.loc.gov/2022024622
LC ebook record available at https://lccn.loc.gov/2022024623

Editorial Credits
Editor: Aaron Sautter; Designer: Elyse White; Media Researcher: Morgan Walters; Production Specialist: Whitney Schaefer

Photo Credit
Getty Images: Bettmann, 29

All internet sites appearing in back matter were available and accurate when this book was sent to press.

Direct quotes appear in **bold, italicized** text on the following pages:

Pages 11, 20, 22, 24, 28 (middle): Salisbury, Gay and Lainey. *The Cruelist Miles: The Heroic Story of Dogs and Men in a Race Against an Epidemic.* New York: W.W. Norton & Company, 2003.
Page 28 (bottom): "Togo," National Park Service, June 29, 2021, https://www.nps.gov/people/togo.htm

TABLE OF CONTENTS

Chapter 1: Dog Town's Greatest Hero

The town of Nome is at the western tip of Alaska, close to the Arctic Circle.

In the early 1900s, the only way to reach Nome in the winter was by dog sled. Dog sleds were very important. They were used to transport goods and people all over the town.

Nome had more sled dogs than people. They roamed the streets when they weren't pulling sleds. Mushers even brought their dogs with them to the tavern.

Sled dogs even helped save lives. In the winter of 1925, several children were sick from a disease called diphtheria.

The disease made it hard to breathe. It was deadly, and it was contagious.

Medicine called antitoxin serum could treat the disease. But supplies were hundreds of miles away. The only way to get the medicine to Nome was by dog sled.

Teams of mushers and their dogs were recruited to deliver the serum to Nome.

One team traveled farther than any other. They also covered the hardest part of the trail.

This team was led by Leonhard Seppala and one heroic dog—Togo.

Chapter 2: King of the Trail

Leonhard Seppala moved to Alaska from Norway in 1900. He worked for a mining company as a musher.

Seppala's team of dogs brought supplies to the mining camps during the winter.

In 1914, Seppala entered his first sled dog race: the All Alaska Sweepstakes.

Are you sure the dogs are ready, Sepp? They're still young. It's a 400-mile race.

Yes, but they're eager, and fast. I know how to guide them.

Seppala's team did well at first. But as they climbed Topkok Mountain, they were hit by a strong blizzard.

I can't even see the lead dogs. But we're close to the top of the mountain. We can't stay up here.

Hike, dogs! Hike! Go!

ARF!

ARF!

ARF!

ARF!

ARF!

ARF!

Oh no! Cliff ahead! Whoa, dogs! Whoa!

WOOF! ARF!

BARK!

WHOA! STOP!

The cliff fell hundreds of feet to the sea below.

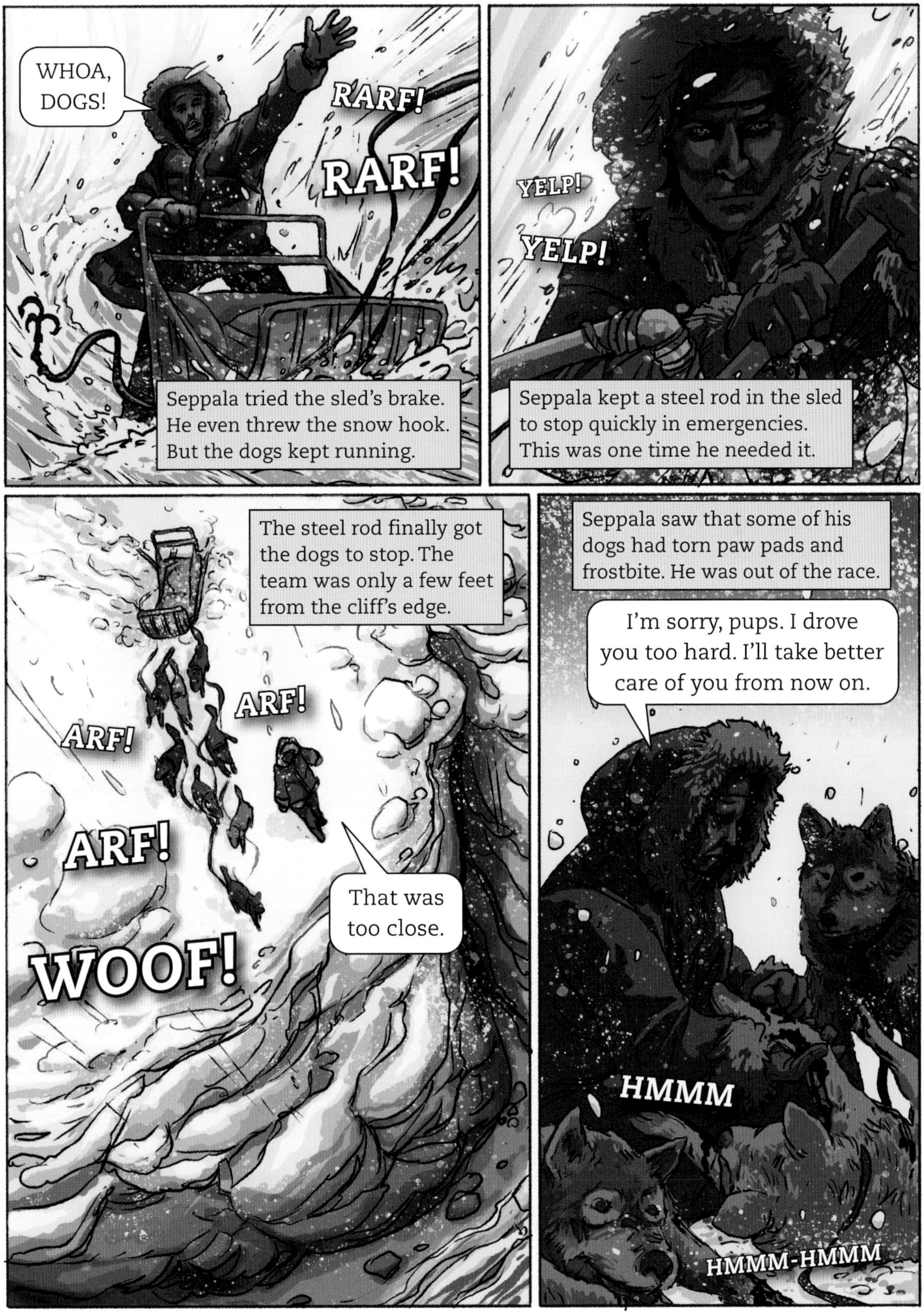
WHOA, DOGS!
RARF!
RARF!
Seppala tried the sled's brake. He even threw the snow hook. But the dogs kept running.
YELP!
YELP!
Seppala kept a steel rod in the sled to stop quickly in emergencies. This was one time he needed it.
The steel rod finally got the dogs to stop. The team was only a few feet from the cliff's edge.
ARF!
ARF!
ARF!
WOOF!
That was too close.
Seppala saw that some of his dogs had torn paw pads and frostbite. He was out of the race.
I'm sorry, pups. I drove you too hard. I'll take better care of you from now on.
HMMM
HMMM-HMMM

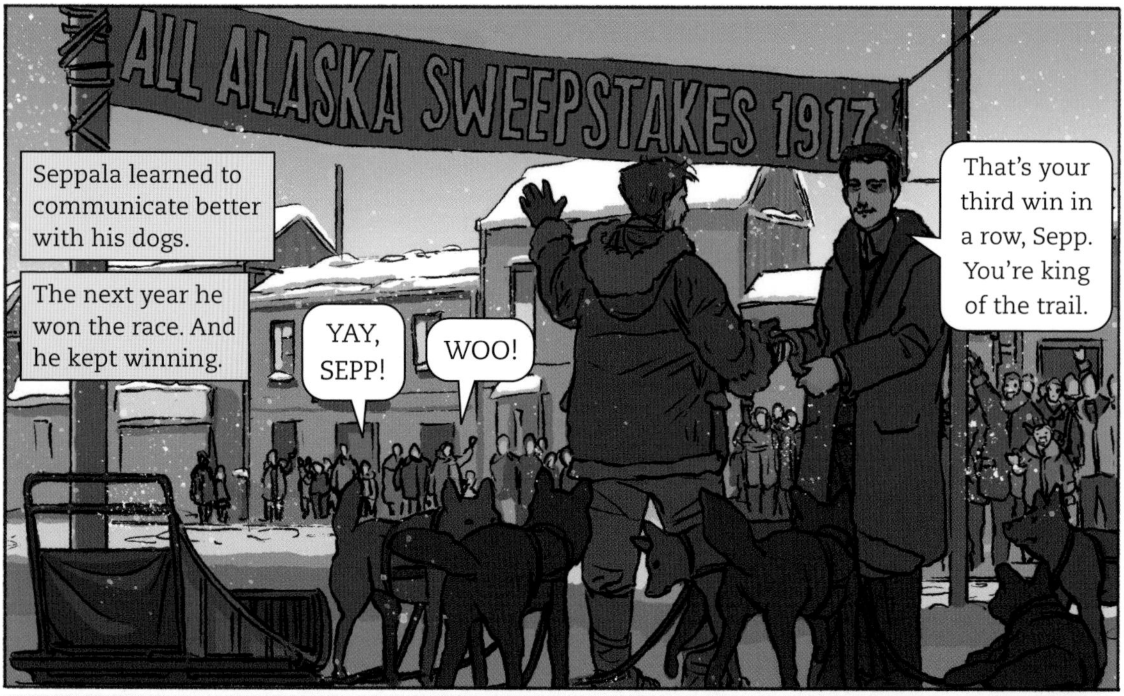
ALL ALASKA SWEEPSTAKES 1917
Seppala learned to communicate better with his dogs.
The next year he won the race. And he kept winning.
YAY, SEPP!
WOO!
That's your third win in a row, Sepp. You're king of the trail.

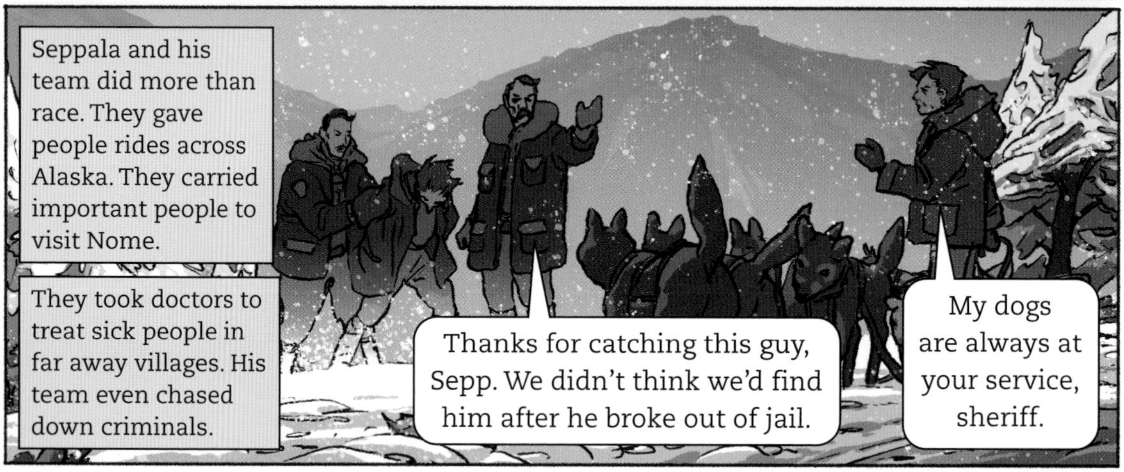
Seppala and his team did more than race. They gave people rides across Alaska. They carried important people to visit Nome.
They took doctors to treat sick people in far away villages. His team even chased down criminals.
Thanks for catching this guy, Sepp. We didn't think we'd find him after he broke out of jail.
My dogs are always at your service, sheriff.

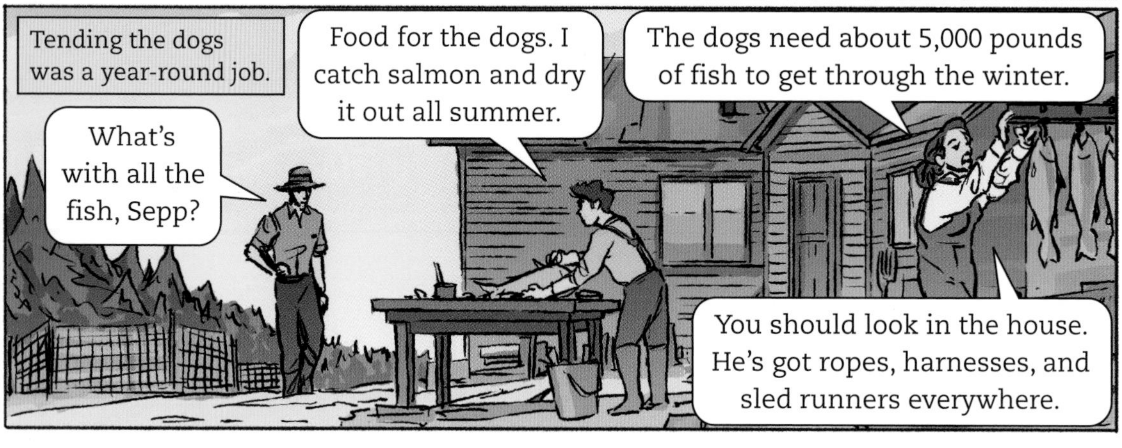
Tending the dogs was a year-round job.
What's with all the fish, Sepp?
Food for the dogs. I catch salmon and dry it out all summer.
The dogs need about 5,000 pounds of fish to get through the winter.
You should look in the house. He's got ropes, harnesses, and sled runners everywhere.

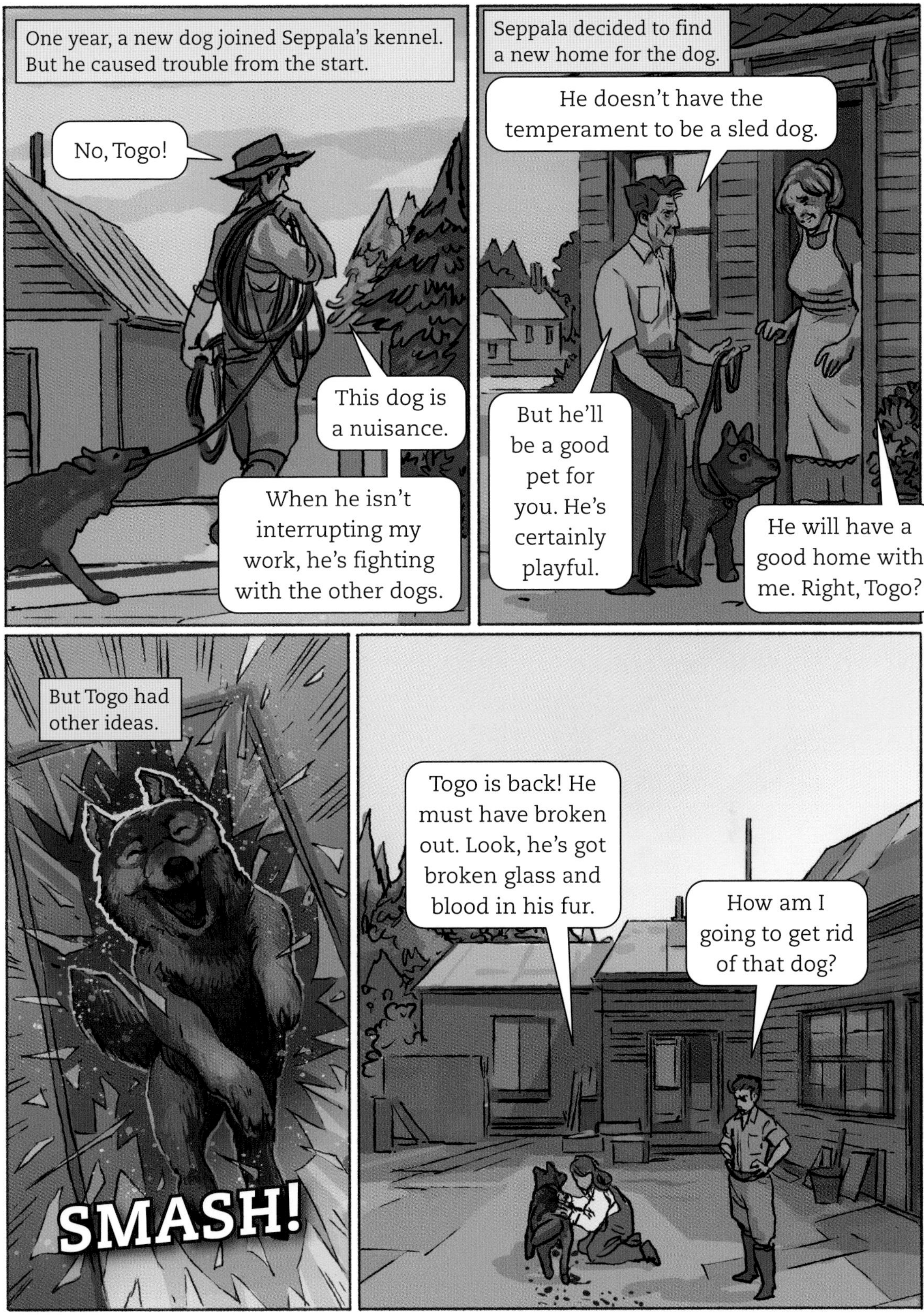
One year, a new dog joined Seppala's kennel. But he caused trouble from the start.
No, Togo!
This dog is a nuisance.
When he isn't interrupting my work, he's fighting with the other dogs.
Seppala decided to find a new home for the dog.
He doesn't have the temperament to be a sled dog.
But he'll be a good pet for you. He's certainly playful.
He will have a good home with me. Right, Togo?
But Togo had other ideas.
SMASH!
Togo is back! He must have broken out. Look, he's got broken glass and blood in his fur.
How am I going to get rid of that dog?

Togo was too rowdy to join the dogsled team. He always nipped at the other dogs.

You're staying here, Togo. We have to run supplies up to Dime Creek. I can't have you bothering the other dogs.

But Togo would not be left behind.

GRRR!

When he tried to jump the kennel fence, the rope got caught at the top.

YIP! YIP!

Hold still, I'm trying to help you.

As soon as he was freed, Togo ran to find his master.

Togo, come back! It's too far!

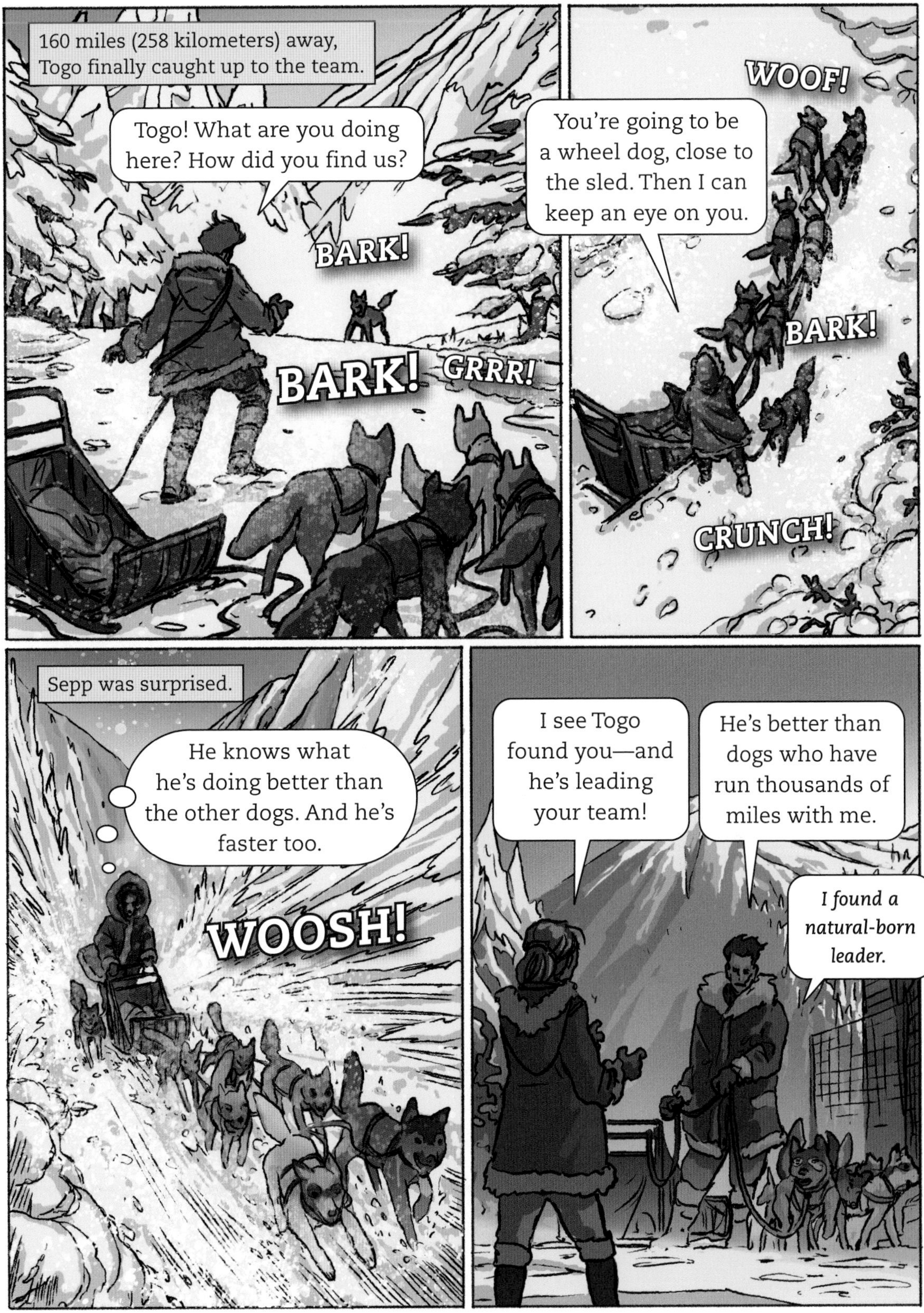
160 miles (258 kilometers) away, Togo finally caught up to the team.
Togo! What are you doing here? How did you find us?
BARK!
BARK!
GRRR!
WOOF!
You're going to be a wheel dog, close to the sled. Then I can keep an eye on you.
BARK!
CRUNCH!
Sepp was surprised.
He knows what he's doing better than the other dogs. And he's faster too.
WOOSH!
I see Togo found you—and he's leading your team!
He's better than dogs who have run thousands of miles with me.
I found a natural-born leader.

Togo was the best lead dog Seppala had ever seen. He trusted Togo with the team. During one long trip, Togo saved the other dogs—and Seppala, too.

Togo was leading the team across the ice of Norton Bay. Suddenly, the ice broke apart.

CRACK!

CRACK!

CRACK!

CRACK!

Seppala and the dogs were trapped on an ice floe. The wind was blowing them away from land.

It's too far across the water for me to jump. You'll have to go over, Togo.

Seppala tied a line to Togo and threw him across the water.

SNAP!

But the line broke.

12

Togo dove into the water to get the broken line.

SPLASH!

Then he climbed back onto the ice to pull the rope.

WOOF!

ARF!

ARF!

Pull, Togo! Pull!

GRRR!

Togo pulled the ice floe across the channel of water. Seppala and the dogs were able to get to the other side.

Good dog, Togo! Good dog! Now let's hook you up and go home.

WOOF!

ARF!

ARF!

Chapter 3: Running to Save Lives

The holiday season was a cheerful time in Nome. The town arranged games and parties for children.

But in January 1925, one young boy missed the festivities. He was sick with a disease that made it hard to breathe.

There are sores in his throat. It's a clear symptom of diphtheria.

An antitoxin serum could treat diphtheria. But Dr. Welch didn't have enough of the medicine to treat the boy.

I'm sorry. I did all I could to help him.

The next morning, Dr. Welch was called out of bed. A local Inuit girl was sick.

She cannot breathe. Please help her, doctor.

Sadly, the little girl died that night.

Dr. Welch asked the mayor to call a meeting of the town council.

Diphtheria is almost always fatal. And it is very contagious. We need people to quarantine right away.

The antitoxin serum can cure the disease. But the nearest supply is in Anchorage.

I don't know how we can get it. That's more than a 1,000-mile round trip.

The sea is frozen. We can't get ships here until spring.

And airplanes have open cockpits. The pilots would freeze to death.

What about the train from Anchorage to Nenana? That's how we get the mail.

Nenana is 674 miles away. It takes a dogsled team 25 days to carry mail from Nenana to Nome.

We need to find someone who can get there fast.

We don't have 25 days. The disease spreads too quickly.

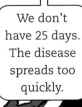

15

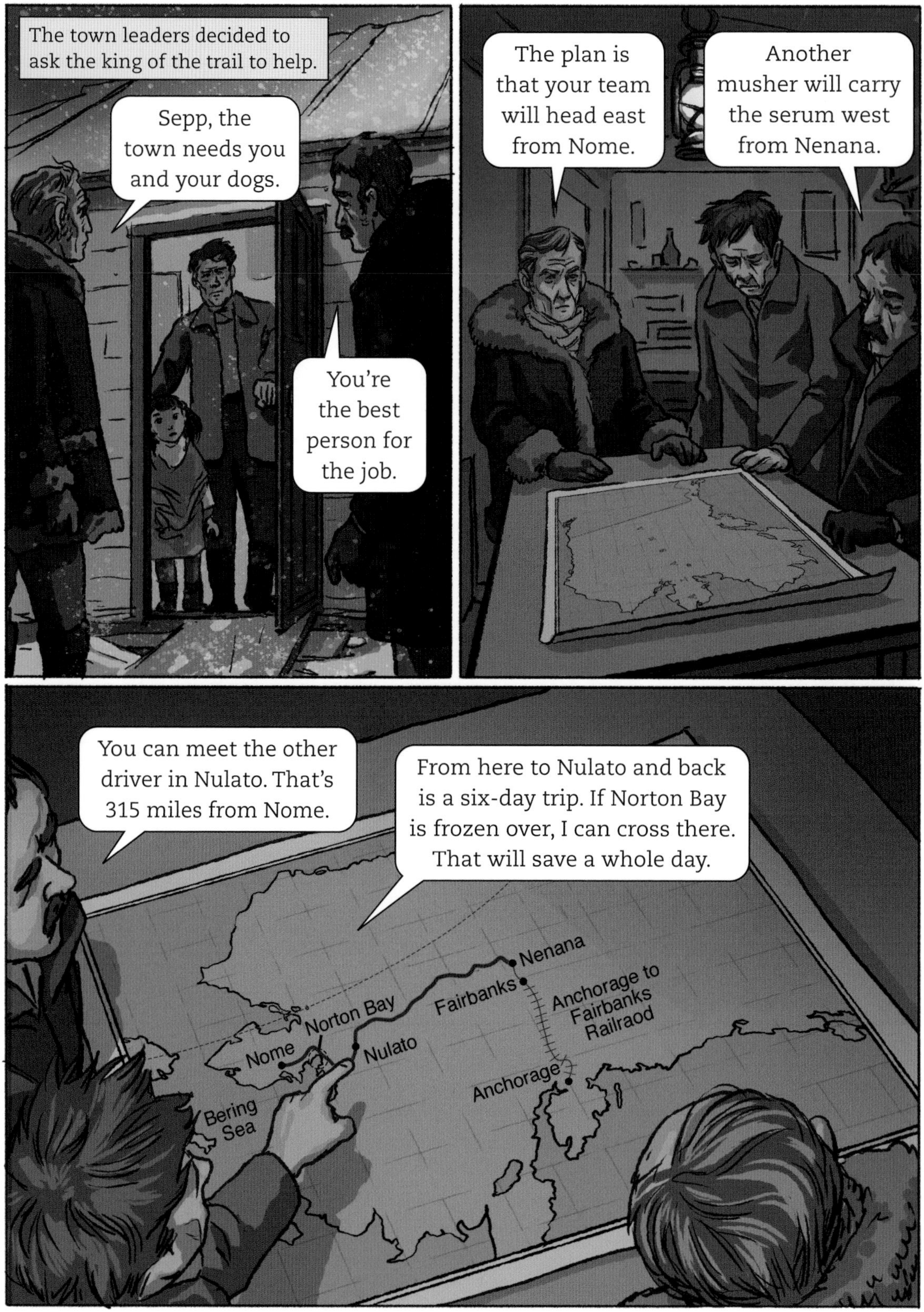
The town leaders decided to ask the king of the trail to help.
Sepp, the town needs you and your dogs.
You're the best person for the job.
The plan is that your team will head east from Nome.
Another musher will carry the serum west from Nenana.
You can meet the other driver in Nulato. That's 315 miles from Nome.
From here to Nulato and back is a six-day trip. If Norton Bay is frozen over, I can cross there. That will save a whole day.
Nenana
Fairbanks
Anchorage to Fairbanks Railraod
Norton Bay
Nome
Nulato
Anchorage
Bering Sea

As Seppala prepared for the journey, the temperature began to drop.

You can't run the dogs if it gets colder than minus 40 degrees.

I know, but I need to go. It's for the town's children—and for Sigrid.

Togo had already led Seppala's team for a long time. He was 12 years old.

Do you have one more long run in you, pup? This will be a fast one. And it will be hard.

The town's children were already in quarantine. But the adults of Nome came out to cheer Seppala's team as they left.

Hike! Hike!

Good dog, Togo!

We'll be waiting for you!

Go Sepp!

WOOF!

ARF!

Chapter 4: A Dangerous Race

That night, 674 miles (1,085 km) from Nome, a crowd waited at the train station in Nenana. Wild Bill Shannon was the best musher in the interior of Alaska. His team, led by Blackie, was ready to go.

The governor sent out a telegram, Bill. Other mushers along the trail have answered the call for volunteers.

You only need to get to Tolovana. Another musher will be waiting there to take the serum.

That's about 50 miles away. I can go through the night and get there by morning.

Here comes the train!

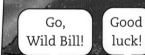

This is precious cargo. There's enough serum to stop the outbreak in Nome.

Make sure you keep it warm, Bill. The medicine can't freeze. And keep yourself warm too. It's getting colder.

I'll tie it down tight on the sled.

Go, Wild Bill!

Good luck!

When Shannon set out, the temperature was already close to minus 50 degrees Fahrenheit (minus 46 degrees Celsius.) His nostrils stung with each breath.

The dogs are too cold. They're not running in rhythm with each other.

And my feet and legs are getting numb.

ARF!

ARF!

Shannon ran ahead of Blackie to keep his legs warm and to keep the team moving. If they stopped, they would die in the cold.

Come on, pups. Come on, Blackie! Keep up with me, boy.

WOOF!

That night the temperature dropped to –62° F (–52° C.) At the Tolovana roadhouse, a Native musher named Edgar Kallands waited to take the serum to the next stop down the trail.

Bill, you need to get inside. Your face is black from frostbite.

Go now. Take the serum. I must tend to my dogs. They're exhausted and hurt.

The cold was too much for Shannon's dogs. Three of them died after the harsh trip.

The roadhouse keeper in Tolovana sent a telegraph message . . .

. . . *Antitoxin departed Tolovana at 11 AM.*

News about the serum run quickly spread across the United States.

San Francisco [...]

DOGS RACE AGAINST DEATH

CHICAGO DAILY JOURNAL

RELAY ACROSS ALASKA

THE PHILADELPHIA RECORD

SLED DOGS RACE TO SAVE ALASKA CHILDREN

THE NEW YORK HERALD.

NEW YORK, SUNDAY MORNING, MAY 3, 1896.

DOGS CARRY SERUM TO SAVE ALASKA TOWN

For the next three days, the relay continued across Alaska. Each team carried the serum about 30 miles (48 km) through forests, over mountains, and along frozen rivers.

Several mushers were Native Alaskans, either Athabascan or Inuit people.

Hike, dogs! Hike!

The cold was fierce. Temperatures dropped to as low as –85° F (–65° C.)

GRRRR!

BARK!

GRRR!

Meanwhile in Nome, more children were getting sick. Dr. Welch had 22 patients with diphtheria. Five children had died since the outbreak began.

The quarantine isn't helping. The disease is still spreading. We need the serum now.

The governor wants to send it by airplane. But it's too risky. There's a storm coming.

We must send out other mushers to help Sepp. His team might be the fastest in Alaska, but Togo and the other dogs will be worn out from the long trip.

I'll ask for volunteers. Each team can wait at a roadhouse on the trail and relay the serum back to Nome.

One of the mushers was Gunnar Kaasen. He worked with Seppala at the mining company.

He didn't have his own dogs, so he used some from Seppala's kennel.

You're putting Balto in the lead with Fox? Sepp doesn't think he's a lead dog.

I've always liked Balto. He's a strong dog.

Chapter 5: Across the Ice

On the fourth day on the trail, Seppala's team reached Norton Bay—the same bay where Togo had saved the team years earlier.

Can you get us across quickly, Togo? There's a storm coming. We don't want to get stuck on the ice again.

WOOF!

Togo and the team dashed across the frozen bay. After crossing the ice, they were close to the next roadhouse.

BARK!

ARF!

BARK!

Good work, Togo! Shaktoolik isn't far ahead. We'll rest there.

What's that? Looks like another team.

It was an Inuit musher named George Ivanoff.

ARF!

BARK!

The serum! The serum! I have it here!

The disease is spreading. They called for more mushers to help. Someone will be waiting for you at Golovin, on the other side of Norton Bay.

Togo and the team had just crossed the ice to beat the storm. Now they had to cross it again—straight into the storm.

It's already too dark to see to the other shore. But we must get across.

You know the way, old friend.

The trip back was 20 miles (32 km) long. Using his sense of smell, Togo followed their previous trail and guided the team back across the ice.

Seppala listened for sounds of the ice cracking. But the ice held firm all the way across.

WOOF!

BARK!

ARFFF!

Togo successfully led the team back across the dangerous ice.

Once on shore, Seppala stopped the team at a roadhouse. Togo and the dogs rested for a few hours before setting off on the last leg of their trip.

We need to get to Golovin tomorrow. It's not far, but we have to go back on the ice along the coast, and then cross the mountains.

The storm is breaking up the ice. *Maybe you should go closer to the shore.*

The Inuit man was right. In the middle of the bay, the storm broke apart the ice they had crossed only a few hours earlier. Seppala kept Togo and the team close to the shoreline.

ARF! ROWF! ARF!

The team turned off the ice and started climbing the mountains. After four and a half days on the trail, Togo and the dogs were close to exhaustion.

They're starting to stumble. Thank goodness I have Togo. He's keeping them going.

Togo led the team to climb more than 5,000 feet (1,500 meters) to the top of the mountains.

There's Golovin. Only a bit further, pups! Then you can have a long rest.

ROWF!

ARF!

At Golovin, Seppala passed the serum to a musher named Charlie Olson.

There are other mushers waiting further down the trail. We'll get the serum to Nome.

With Togo in the lead, Seppala's team traveled 170 miles (274 km) from Nome to Shaktoolik. They then turned around and raced 91 miles (147 km) with the serum to Golovin.

In just four and a half days, Togo led the team across 261 miles (420 km) of rough Alaskan wilderness. Seppala's dogs traveled more than 200 miles (322 km) farther than any other team in the 1925 serum run.

ALASKA

NORTON BAY

NOME:
Leaves on January 28

GOLOVIN:
Passes serum to next musher on February 1

SHAKTOOLIK:
Receives serum on January 31

NORTON SOUND

Chapter 6: When Dogs Saved Children

The relay wasn't over. The mushers and dogs still had to take the serum the last 78 miles (126 km) back to Nome. And the storm was getting stronger. The winds blew Charlie Olson's team off the trail.

WHIMMM-HMMM

HMMM

The wind is too strong! I have to wrap you pups up against the cold. Then we'll get back on the trail.

That night, Olson reached the next roadhouse. Gunnar Kaasen was waiting.

Your dogs are fed and resting. They wouldn't have lasted much longer.

Even with two parkas on, I was freezing. You'll have to wait out the storm, Gunnar.

My dogs are ready to go. If I wait too long, the trail will be covered with snow drifts.

Be careful. This is the worst blizzard I've seen.

Whoa, dogs! Balto, stop!

ARF!

ROWF!

It was the worst blizzard in years. On the forest trail, Kaasen's team fought through deep snow drifts. Then after leaving the woods, they were hit by winds off the ocean.

Wind gusts howled at more than 70 miles (113 km) per hour. The winds tipped over Kaasen's sled. The serum was knocked from the sled.

Where is it? WHERE IS IT?

Here it is! Thank goodness!

Early the next morning, Kaasen and his team arrived in Nome. The relay was finished.

He made it!

It's here! The serum is here!

We need to warm it up.

Is it Sepp?

No, it's Gunnar Kaasen.

You're a fine dog, Balto.

The serum arrived just in time. The diphtheria had started to spread to the children's parents. The medicine stopped the outbreak.

News of the Alaska serum run quickly spread across the country. Gunnar Kaasen and Balto became famous.

Did you hear? Gunnar and Balto have left for Hollywood. They're going to be in a movie.

Gunnar didn't want to do it. He's very shy. He doesn't like all the attention.

I don't care about Gunnar getting famous. *We all did our best.* But putting Balto in a movie? *If any dog deserved special mention, it was Togo.*

After the serum run, Togo no longer made long runs through the Alaska winter. He and Seppala moved to Maine where he lived happily for the rest of his life. Togo died in 1929 at the age of 16.

When he was an old man, Leonhard Seppala still remembered his favorite dog. "*I never had a better dog than Togo,*" Sepp said.

Togo's Legacy

With Togo in the lead, Seppala's dogs traveled farther than any other team in the 1925 serum run. On a single day, when they crossed over Norton Bay and back, Togo led his team for 84 miles (135 km)—more than any other team traveled in the entire relay.

Seppala and Togo

After Seppala and Togo moved to Maine in 1926, a woman there bought Togo and the rest of Seppala's team. She wanted to breed and raise sled dogs. Sepp helped manage the kennel for her.

Togo was a Siberian Husky. His puppies were the start of a new breed, called Seppala Siberian Sleddogs.

A statue of the brave sled dog was placed in New York City's Seward Park in 2001. In 2011, TIME *Magazine* named Togo the most heroic animal ever.

In 2019, Togo was the subject of a new Disney film. In the movie, Togo was played by a dog named Diesel. He is a Seppala Siberian Sleddog and one of Togo's direct descendents.

Glossary

antitoxin serum
(an-tee-TAHK-suhn SIHR-uhm)
a liquid medicine used to fight a contagious disease or immunize people

contagious
(kuhn-TEY-juhs)
able to quickly spread from one person to another

diphtheria
(dif-THEER-ee-uh)
a serious infection that creates a thick gray membrane in a person's throat, making it very hard to breathe

frostbite (FRAWST-byte)
an injury resulting from parts of the body being exposed to extreme cold

kennel (KEN-uhl)
an organization or business that breeds and trains dogs

nuisance (NOO-suhns)
someone or something that is annoying or obnoxious

quarantine
(KWOR-uhn-teen)
to keep a person away from others to stop a disease from spreading

recruit (rih-KROOT)
to ask people to help with a task or join a group

relay (REE-lay)
an event in which someone carries an object over a certain distance and then gives it to another person who carries it to the next handoff spot

symptom (SIMP-tuhm)
a sign that shows that a person is sick with a disease or health problem

temperament
(TEM-pur-uh-muhnt)
the combination of behavior and personality traits of a person or animal

volunteer (vol-uhn-TEER)
someone who offers to do a task without pay

Read More

Berne, Emma Carlson. *Balto*. New York: Scholastic Press, 2022.

Mikoley, Kate. *The Iditarod*. New York: Gareth Stevens Publishing, 2021.

Parachini, Jodie. *Togo and Balto: The Dogs Who Saved a Town*. Chicago: Albert Whitman and Company, 2022.

Internet Sites

Four Legged Leaders: The Serum Run Dogs
youtube.com/watch?v=l3PMGfUGMoc

National Park Service: Togo
nps.gov/people/togo.htm

American Kennel Club: The True Story of Togo
akc.org/expert-advice/news/togo-siberian-husky-sled-dog-hero-of-1925/

About the Author

Bruce Berglund was a history professor for 19 years. He taught courses on ancient and modern history, war and society, and sports. He has traveled to many countries to research history books. He lives in Minnesota and loves winter. He often goes snowshoeing on cold winter days.

About the Illustrator

Dante Ginevra is a versatile cartoonist, illustrator and art director, from Buenos Aires, Argentina. Since 1999, he has published several comic books and graphic novels in Argentina, Uruguay, Brazil, France, Spain, Italy, England, the United States and Canada; some of these include: *La Malédiction de L'immortel, Malandras, Los Dueños de la Tierra, El Muertero Zabaletta, El Asco*. Dante has also worked as a teacher in Argentine Universities. For more information visit: www.danteginevra.com.